Peak District
PANORAMAS

SIMON KIRWAN

TEXT: JEROME MONAHAN

MYRIAD
LONDON

CONTENTS

THE NORTH PEAKS

The North Peaks – often known as the 'Dark Peak' – contain the brooding gritstone moors of Kinder and Bleaklow as well as the picturesque but remote Ladybower and Derwent reservoirs

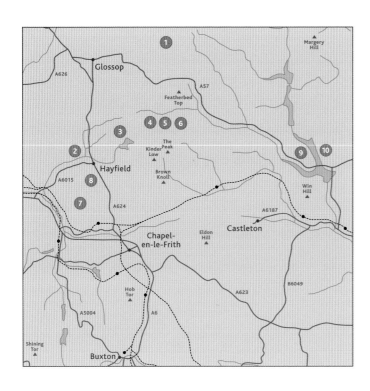

OPPOSITE – THE PENNINE WAY
The Old Nag's Head, Edale, is the traditional starting point for walkers setting off on this long-distance footpath

BLEAKLOW

Bleaklow's underlying impermeable millstone grit has prevented water drainage for millennia, creating one of the most stunning peat bog areas in Europe. Here is the largest area of land above 2000ft (609m) in England. The landscape is criss-crossed by deep drainage channels called 'groughs' (pronounced 'gruffs') and high banks of peat called 'hags'. It can be an uncanny place. The writer and fell-walker Alfred Wainwright said of this area 'it is certainly mucky, too often belaboured by wind and rain', adding, 'cheer up – there's worse to come'.

HAYFIELD VILLAGE

In the Domesday Book the town was referred to as 'Hedfeld'. Its main river is the Sett which has been a key element in Hayfield's industrial past. It is hard to believe wandering this picturesque place that it was once a home to wool and cotton manufacture, papermaking and textile printing. In 1932, Hayfield cricket ground was the meeting place of 400 ramblers intent on performing a mass trespass on Kinder Scout – a key moment in the 'right to roam' campaign.

KINDER RESERVOIR

Construction of the Kinder Reservoir and its much-photographed circular filter house was completed in 1911. Built from local stone and clay, the reservoir was created to supply nearby Stockport. It reduced the flow of the Sett and ended its periodic flooding of Hayfield. In order to transport the building materials to this remote spot, a special railway spur was created but the two-mile track and the 'tin town' of workers' shacks that sprang up just north of Bowden Bridge have both vanished now.

KINDER SUMMIT

Once this was common land – a place for grazing, peat-cutting and light quarrying. Then, in 1836, Kinder Scout was declared off-limits by an Act of Enclosure. That we can now wander this stunning spot – a 15 mile (24km) plateau of peat bogs and groughs, some resembling First World War trenches – is thanks in large part to 400 walkers and their mass trespass of April 24 1932. The event was specifically mentioned in the 1945 Dower Report that led to the creation of the UK's national parks.

KINDER SCOUT – WESTERN EDGE

The northern Dark Peaks are a landscape of 'brooding tablelands' punctured by craggy valleys marked by steep drops frequently referred to as 'edges'.
It is here that the walker may well catch sight of buzzards or, if they are lucky, one of the peregrine falcons that are making a comeback to the region.
Bleak it can be, bare and eroded too, but Kinder also boasts a wide range of habitats including upland heath, grassland and bracken – each its own
unique eco-system.

KINDER DOWNFALL

Kinder Scout is thought to derive its name from the Saxon words for 'water over the edge' or *Kyndwr Scut*. Nowhere is this more appropriate than at Kinder Downfall, where most of the plateau's water gathers to drop over 98ft (30m). In windy conditions, the famous 'blow back' effect occurs, with the water being diverted skyward. In the winter the flow can freeze, creating a ribbon of refracting silver against the dark slopes of the Kinder Downfall amphitheatre.

LOOKING NORTH FROM CHINLEY CHURN

The actual triangulation point at Chinley Churn 1479ft (451m) is currently off-limits, though the surrounding area remains popular with walkers and mountain-bikers. The village of Hayfield developed at the site of several Roman routes and was also a key staging post for packhorses in the Middle Ages. The steeple of St Matthew's Church is visible. Periodic flooding of the Sett has cost Hayfield several bridges and in 1748 even swept the dead from their graves in St Matthew's churchyard.

LOOKING WEST FROM PEEP O'DAY

Peep O' Day is a farmhouse boasting an attractive porch topped by a small window. It is through this that the sun shines at break of day onto the interior stairway and, it is suggested, provides the source for the building's unusual name. It is reached via a steeply climbing road that once was the main route between Chinley and Hayfield – that status now ceded to the nearby A624. The fields and pastures here are bounded by higher more exposed ground such as Mount Famine to the east.

LADYBOWER RESERVOIR

The Ladybower is one of three reservoirs constructed in the Upper Derwent Valley to supply water to Sheffield, Derby, Nottingham and Leicester. It was built between 1935 and 1943 and contains over 6000 million gallons (27,276 million litres) of water. The reservoir flooded the villages of Derwent and Ashopton. Much of the stone of Derwent's houses went to reinforce the dam, and Ashopton's site provides the foundations for the viaduct that carries the A57 over the reservoir's expanse. The reservoir is home to still water trout farming.

DERWENT MOORS FROM LADYBOWER

The Derwent Reservoir is formed by one of the 'three dams' that help store the water of the Upper Derwent – the others are Ladybower and Howden. It was here that 617 Squadron under Wing Commander Guy Gibson flew practice sorties before their successful mission in 1943 to bomb the Mohne and Eder dams. The dam's association with this famous exploit continues to be a tourist draw. Legend has it that the bells of Derwent's village church, drowned by the reservoir's waters, can still be heard. Its steeple can be seen in periods of drought.

THE CENTRAL PEAKS

The Central Peaks, between Castleton and Bakewell, is a beautiful region of rolling countryside overlooked
by high dramatic ridges and rocky peaks

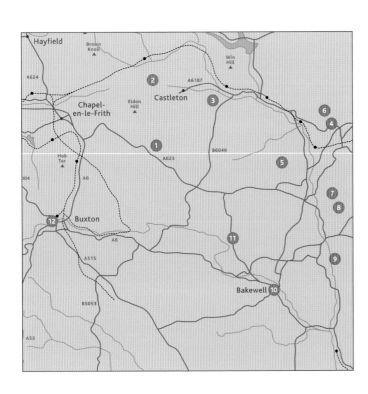

OPPOSITE – PAVILION GARDENS, BUXTON
The beautifully restored Octagon and Paxton Suite is the perfect setting for refreshments on a summer morning

PEAK FOREST

'Forest' is a misnomer as this is not a heavily wooded area, though its open parkland gained it the status of a Royal Forest in the Middle Ages. The local church was built in 1657 and is dedicated, unusually, to King Charles the Martyr. Its location in a Royal Forest gave its vicar special powers, enabling him to marry couples from outside the parish without the customary prior reading of Banns. The practice was ended in 1804 by Act of Parliament, for being 'productive of Bad Consequencies'.

MAM TOR AND THE GREAT RIDGE

The National Trust has laid flagstones to protect the Great Ridge that culminates in Mam Tor at the head of Hope Valley. Mam Tor itself climbs spectacularly to 1696ft (517m). Its unstable rock structure results in rock falls. It is called locally 'the Shivering Mountain'. Charles Cotton considered it one of the seven wonders of the Peak District in his travel book of 1681. Below Mam Tor, the A625 used to be a main trans-Pennine route until a landslip in 1977 led to its permanent closure to traffic.

CAVEDALE

The sheer sides of Cavedale helped make the Norman Peveril Castle impregnable. It was built in 1080 by William Peverel, claimed to be the illegitimate son of William the Conquerer. The castle defended the royal hunting grounds in the area and also the local lead-mining industry but it fell into decline in Tudor times. Peak Cavern Gorge on its west side is over 230ft (70m) deep and its huge entrance arch – long considered a wonder of the Peak District – is known as the 'Devil's Arse'.

STANAGE EDGE

Overlooking the Derwent valley, Stanage is the most impressive of the Peak District's gritstone edges. The entire ridge is approximately 3.5 miles long from its northern tip to the southern point near the Cowper Stone. The highest point on Stanage Edge is High Neb which reaches a height of 1502ft (458m). Stanage is a popular spot for climbing and some of the more challenging sections have been given fanciful names such as Marble Wall, the Tower, Black Hawk and Robin Hood's Cave.

EYAM MOOR AND DERWENT VALLEY

When the plague struck Eyam in 1665, brought there in a box of cloth or clothes from London, the village's rector, the Rev William Mompesson and a local man, Thomas Stanley, persuaded the entire community to place itself in quarantine and thus managed to stop its spread to the surrounding area. Over two years 259 villagers died and many of the houses bear plaques commemorating individuals who succumbed to the disease. In August every year a thanksgiving service is held in a limestone 'delph' called Cucklett Church to mark their sacrifice.

OVER OWLER TOR

Over Owler Tor lies about 1246ft (380m) above sea level and gives spectacular views of the surrounding 'rounded' landscape. From the summit, the town of Hathersage and the Derwent are visible to the north-west. Parts of the Hope Valley near Hathersage are thought to have been the inspiration for some of *Jane Eyre*. Charlotte Bronte was a friend of Ellen Nussey, whose brother was the vicar of Hathersage, and she was their visitor in 1845.

CURBAR EDGE

Curbar Edge is part of a unique 12 mile (19km) gritstone escarpment marking the eastern side of the Derwent Valley. This is one of the most popular areas in the Peaks for climbing and many of the routes enjoy colourful nicknames including 'homicide', 'don't slip now' and 'knockin' on heaven's door'. The photograph shows a view north towards Froggatt Edge. Far below are the villages of Curbar and Calver where the local cotton mill was used to recreate Colditz Castle for a television series.

BASLOW EDGE

Baslow Edge is a key point on the famous gritstone escarpment fringing the Derwent Valley. On the escarpment is the 1866 commemorative cross for the Duke of Wellington in recognition of his victory over Napoleon at Waterloo. Here too is the Eagle Stone – a massive block of gritstone. According to tradition, young men from Baslow had to climb the stone as a rite of passage, proving themselves worthy of marriage. The photograph shows a southerly view down the Derwent Valley looking in the direction of Chatsworth House.

CHATSWORTH

Often referred to as 'the Palace of the Peaks', Chatsworth is one of the finest stately homes in Britain. The present house was built by the first Duke of Devonshire between 1686 and 1707. The magnificent grounds are the work of two men of genius: Lancelot 'Capability' Brown who landscaped the grounds to create a 'natural' parkland setting in the 18th century and Joseph Paxton who, in the 19th century, added the garden structures and water features.

HOLME BRIDGE BAKEWELL

The busy market town of Bakewell is the unofficial capital of the Eastern Peaks. Holme Bridge, the historic five-arch packhorse bridge which spans the river Wye dates from 1664. There was a ford at this point which had long been used as a river crossing by wool drovers and merchants. Close by is Lumford Mill, originally built as a cotton-spinning mill in 1778 by Sir Richard Arkwright. Many of the adjoining cottages were constructed for mill-workers.

SHEEPWASH BRIDGE ASHFORD

This medieval three-arch bridge is a favourite with visitors to Ashford-in-the-Water, a quiet and idyllic village on the river Wye. A small enclosure nearby gives a clue to the name of the bridge – sheep were flung into the river from the bridge to clean their fleeces before shearing. Ashford became famous for the production of black marble, beloved by the Victorians.

PAVILION GARDENS BUXTON

At the heart of the elegant spa town of Buxton are the Pavilion Gardens, a beautiful 23 acre site designed in 1871 by landscape gardener Edward Milner, who worked with Joseph Paxton. Recently restored to their former glory, the gardens are home to the impressive concert hall called the Octagon and the adjoining Paxton Suite (both just visible through the trees). One of the highlights of the gardens is the splendid Pavilion Hothouse.

THE EAST PEAKS

The East Peaks around Matlock and Middleton contain many traces of the area's former industrial glory,
particularly stone-quarrying, mining and mill-working

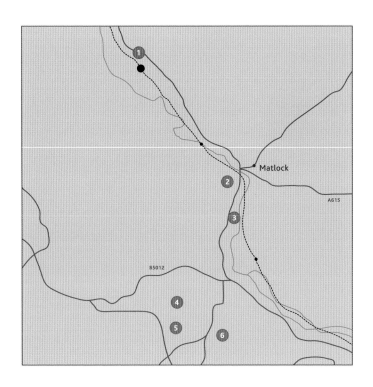

OPPOSITE – HADDON HALL
Thought by many to be the most romantic in England, the garden at Haddon Hall is particularly famed for its collection of roses

PEAK RAIL

A train steams through Darley Dale, one of the stations on the Peak Rail, part of the old Midland Railway which closed in 1968. The Peak Railway Society run regular steam and diesel trains between Matlock Riverside and Rowsley. Beyond Rowsley the beautiful Monsal Dale Trail follows part of the track of the disused railway and includes the dramatic five-arch Monsal Viaduct which carried the railway over the river Wye.

MATLOCK FROM THE HEIGHTS OF ABRAHAM

Matlock marks the southern entrance to the Peak District. It is a busy centre, though this can be forgotten by those braving a cable car up the nearby Heights of Abraham to explore the quiet woodland or the show caves of Great Rutland and the Great Masson Cavern. Another attraction on the Heights is Gulliver's Kingdom theme park. Matlock's fame rests in recent times on its health hydro developed by entrepreneur John Smedley after 1853. By 1867 the hydro was catering for 2000 visitors a year.

RIVER DERWENT

Draining down from the bleak uplands of the northern Peaks, the river Derwent runs down the eastern edge of the Peak District. Its power was harnessed by the pioneers of the Industrial Revolution, including Sir Richard Arkwright who built mills at Cromford and Matlock. This rich history is celebrated in the Derwent Valley Mills World Heritage Site, with Masson Mills, near Matlock Bath, at its centre.

MIDDLETON TOP

Middleton Top gives the visitor impressive views of the Derwent Valley, north towards Matlock Bath. During the later stages of the Industrial Revolution, 'The Top' was chosen as the pivotal point in an unusual transport link between Cromford Canal and the Peak Forest Canal. It was here that the 33 mile (53km) long Cromford and High Peak Railway was built in 1830, following canal-like construction with flat sections and steep inclines. The Middleton Top engine house housed the steam-winding equipment used to pull the wagons up the 1-in-8 gradient.

MIDDLETON QUARRY

Middleton Quarry is one of many sites of former limestone extraction now returning to nature. It lies to the south of Middleton Moor and is now a popular site with walkers, rider, climbers and mountain bikers, lying on the route of the 17.5 mile (28km) High Peak Trail. As well as this quarry, the Trail also boasts reminders of this area's industrial heritage such as old engine houses, sidings and signals. Middleton was made famous by DH Lawrence who located his short novel *The Virgin and the Gypsy* here, renaming the village Woodlinkin.

CROMFORD

In the past, Cromford's fortunes have been associated with the Wye. Its waters had long been used to power flour mills but in the 18th century their energy was turned to industrial purposes driving the machinery of the first water-powered cotton-spinning mill designed by Richard Arkwright. It was built in 1772 and helped make Arkwright a fortune, some of which he ploughed into local building-workers' cottages and a school. Cromford has been described as one of England's first purpose-built industrial villages.

THE SOUTH PEAKS

A contrast to the bleaker moors of the north, the South Peaks is an area of beautiful undulating green dales interspersed with limestone gorges such as the Dove valley

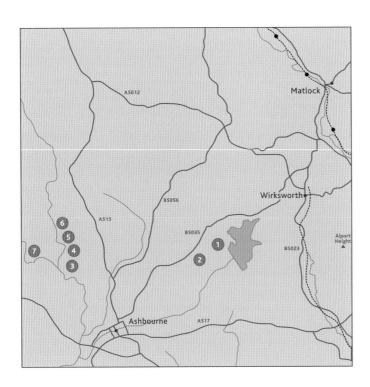

OPPOSITE – ASHBOURNE
Known as the 'gateway to Dovedale' the pretty market town of Ashbourne is famous for its annual Shrove Tuesday football game played between two huge local teams

CARSINGTON WATER

Carsington Water has become a big attraction since its opening in 1992. The reservoir is owned and operated by Severn Trent Water and it takes and stores water pumped from the River Derwent at times of high rainfall. The reservoir's visitors' centre contains a permanent exhibition explaining the essential role water plays in our lives. In the courtyard is the Kugel Stone, a ball of granite weighing over 1 tonne and which revolves on a thin film of water under pressure.

SOUTH DERBYSHIRE DALES

This area, south of Carsington Water and near the villages of Hognaston and Kirk Ireton, became prominent in the 17th century because of its location on the main route between London and Manchester. Today, the once busy villages are much quieter thanks to the new by-pass built to accommodate traffic to the reservoir. Both villages boast fine old churches. At Holy Trinity Church in Kirk Ireton, the convention is for children to rope off the road, preventing a just-married couple's departure until they have paid a toll.

BUNSTER HILL

Bunster Hill and Thorpe Cloud are prominent summits carved out of the landscape's limestone thanks to glacial and post-glacial erosion. Both peaks climb to over 984ft (300m). It is here that the River Dove moves from Dovedale into Lin Dale, the spot marked in the valley below by a set of stepping stones. Opposite Bunster Hill is Lover's Leap – a cliff from which a jilted girl threw herself in despair, only to have her fall cushioned by the bushes below.

LIN DALE

Thorpe Cloud hill, with its conical summit, is one of the most distinctive sites in this region. This is an area in which the bestowing of fanciful names really takes off. Other local peaks include The Twelve Apostles and Tissington Spires. The 19th-century diarist James Thorne felt that Derbyshire people had a genius for naming things. Below Thorpe Cloud is the village of Thorpe, its name originating from the Norse word for an outlying farm or hamlet.

SHAPLOW

At the southern end of Dovedale lies Shaplow Dale, an area specifically designated for rock climbing by the National Trust. It is an area of exceptional beauty lying between Tissington Spires and Reynard's Cave. On the valley slopes opposite can be seen Dovedale Woods – one of the UK's most important remaining ash woods and one key reason why Dovedale was considered for National Park status as early as the 1930s. Eventually Dovedale Woods was incorporated within the Peak District National Park when it was created in 1951.

DOVEDALE

The River Dove derives its name from the old English word 'dubo' meaning 'dark'. It runs southwards for 45 miles (72km) until it enters the River Trent.
It often marks the border between the contrasting limestone and shale geology of Derbyshire and Staffordshire. Even in the Victorian era it was a popular
touring area and it remains one of the most visited parts of the Park. Dr Johnson, an even earlier tourist, suggested that having seen Dovedale there was
no need to go to the Highlands of Scotland.

ILAM

The pretty village of Ilam at the southern end of Dovedale was built in the 1820s in the distinctive Alpine style by the industrialist Jesse Watts-Russell. The village was originally sited near Ilam Hall, shown in the photograph with the church of the Holy Cross behind. The village is a great favourite with visitors – its attractions include the beautiful parkland around the hall and the aptly named Paradise Walk along the banks of the river Manifold.

THE WEST PEAKS

Within easy reach of Manchester, a mix of picturesque moors, placid reservoirs and dramatic gritstone edges make the West Peaks a magnet for visitors

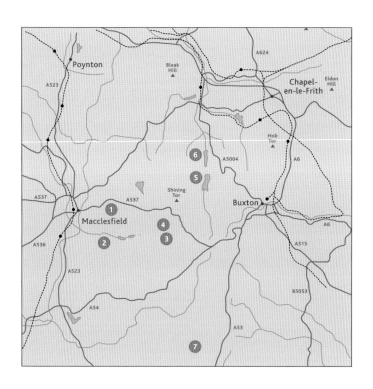

OPPOSITE – THE ROACHES

The Roaches are part of a group of rocky escarpments or 'edges' that stand like sentinels guarding the south-west boundary of the Peak District

TEGG'S NOSE

Tegg's Nose lies just east of Macclesfield. The summit is over 1148ft (350m) and the view west towards the Macclesfield Forest is spectacular. Walkers in
Tegg's Nose Country Park can see as far as the Jodrell Bank telescope, Macclesfield and Bollington. There is a nature trail here that takes visitors past
meadows filled in season with mountain pansies and woodland rich with birdsong all year round. A major drystone wall rebuilding project began here in
2002 using local stone and teams of volunteers including school and community groups.

BOTTOMS RESERVOIR

Over 85 per cent of the north-west's fresh water derives from the region's rivers, lakes and reservoirs. As well as the vast Derwent and Ladybower waters, there are more modest reserves such as that created at Bottoms near the picturesque village of Langley, which helps to control supply in the River Bollin. The reservoir capitalises on its leisure potential. Walkers can enjoy lakeside walks while the perch, bream, carp and tench in the reservoir itself provide plenty of good fishing.

AXE EDGE MOOR

The rivers Dove, Manifold and Goyt all have their sources on Axe Edge Moor. Where the Dove bubbles to the surface is a commemorative stone carrying the names Izaak Walton and Charles Cotton. Walton's *The Compleat Angler* was published in 1653; the Dove was one of his favourite fishing haunts. Cotton was Walton's companion and contributed a chapter on fly fishing to the fifth edition of the book. Once on Axe Edge Moor walking is fairly easy and from there the view encompasses the distinctive summit of Shuttlingsloe – the 'Cheshire Matterhorn'.

TORGATE HILL

To the West of Torgate Hill the view is dominated by trees – the easternmost edge of Macclesfield Forest. It was once a royal hunting ground, more open than today and home to boar, wolves and even bear. Now, the largest mammals are red, roe and fallow deer. The forest is a working area and because the timber is felled and replanted, the woodland scenery is always in a state of change. Opposite Torgate Hill is the village of Macclesfield Forest boasting an historic woodland chapel.

GOYT VALLEY

The River Goyt drains off Axe Edge Moor and flows north, feeding both the Fernilee and Errwood reservoirs en route. The building of these reservoirs in 1938 and 1964 led to the relocation of the 300-year-old Goyt Bridge, an historic packhorse route, further down the valley. In the 1950s this area, like most of the Peaks, saw a decline in the numbers of hunting birds. In recent years the populations have recovered and, in 1997, hen harriers returned to the Goyt Valley.

ERRWOOD RESERVOIR

The Errwood Reservoir was bult to supplement the water supply provided by the Fernilee Reservoir to the city of Stockport. It is a much-visited area and the reservoir frequently bristles with sails and there are many picnic spots along its banks. The nearby Errwood Hall, owned by the Catholic Grimshaw family, was largely demolished at the time of the reservoir's construction, but its chapel and graveyard survive. The area is subject to strict vehicle controls as part of a visitor management system pioneered here and copied on reservoirs elsewhere in the Peaks.

THE ROACHES

The Roaches, with Hen Cloud and Ramshaw Rocks, form a gritstone escarpment which marks the south-western edge of the Peak. This is an area under particular
pressure from visitors. The paths are popular with walkers, the cliffs with climbers and the sky with hang-gliding enthusiasts. The names
of some of the cliff routes known to climbers are colourful including Saul's Crack, Valkyrie and the Mangler. Up top the landscape is dominated by weirdly-shaped
rocks and there are spectacular views of Tittesworth Reservoir and Leek.

First published in 2005 by Myriad Books Limited 35 Bishopsthorpe Road London SE26 4PA

This edition published in 2009.

Photographs copyright © Simon Kirwan   Text copyright © Jerome Monahan

Simon Kirwan has asserted his right under the Copyright, Designs and Patents Act 1998 to be identified as the author of this work.

ISBN 1 904 736 08 4   Designed by Phillip Appleton   Printed in China   www.myriadbooks.com